THANKSGIVING

An Easy-Read Holiday Book

THANKSGIVING

by Cass R. Sandak

illustrations by Carla Bauer

FRANKLIN WATTS
New York/London/Toronto/Sydney
1980
A GROLIER COMPANY

To Mother and Father,
who taught me to be thankful

R.L. 2.9 Spache Revised Formula

Library of Congress Cataloging in Publication Data

Sandak, Cass R.
  Thanksgiving.

  (An Easy-read holiday book)
  Includes index.
  SUMMARY: Discusses the history and meaning
of the Thanksgiving holiday, how it was celebrated
in the past, and how we observe it today.
  1. Thanksgiving Day—Juvenile literature.
[1. Thanksgiving Day] I. Bauer, Carla. II. Title.
III. Series: Easy-read holiday book.
GT4975.S26   394.2′683   80–10583
ISBN 0-531-04150-6

Thanksgiving Day is an American holiday. It began in this country and it is celebrated only by Americans. It is a time to be proud that you are an American. The faith and hard work of the early settlers helped to make our country strong. We can all give thanks for the many good things that Americans share.

Thanksgiving Day may be observed with services in places of worship and with family gatherings around festive dinner tables. Often churches and other groups have Thanksgiving dinners for people who are poor or have no families. It is a time to share with others.

Before the holiday, schools may present pageants or plays showing how the early settlers celebrated the first Thanksgiving.

Christmas, Easter, and even Halloween are hundreds and hundreds of years old. But our modern American Thanksgiving started in **Massachusetts** (Mass-uh-CHEW-sets) about three hundred and sixty years ago.

The full story of the holiday begins almost four hundred years ago in England. The town of **Scrooby** was the center of a religious group called the Pilgrims. The word **pilgrim** means someone who travels for religious reasons.

The Pilgrims wanted a very simple kind of worship. However, in those days it was dangerous to have ideas that were not the same as those of the Church of England.

8

So in 1608 a group of Pilgrims moved to Holland. The Dutch there let people worship as they wished.

The Pilgrims were happy in Holland and stayed until 1620. But they did not like their children growing up in a foreign country. The language was strange and so were the customs. They wanted their children to be English. So the Pilgrims returned to England. There they made plans to settle in the New World.

In the summer of 1620, two ships filled
with Pilgrims sailed from the English port of
Southampton. These ships were the *Mayflower*
and the *Speedwell*. After a few days the *Speedwell*
began to leak badly. Both ships returned to land.
Some of the Pilgrims decided to stay in England.
Others crowded onto the *Mayflower*. Once
again, the ship set sail, this time from the city
of **Plymouth** (PLIM-uth).

10

After a two-month voyage, about one hundred Pilgrims reached the coast of Massachusetts. They were the first English people to settle in that part of America, which they named New England. The Pilgrims landed at a spot now called Plymouth Rock in December 1620. They had no homes and there was very little food. The winter in America was colder than in England. At one point only seven of the Pilgrims were well enough to care for all those who were ill. In that first hard winter, half the Pilgrims died.

The Pilgrims did not know what to expect from the Indians who were already in Massachusetts. They were afraid of surprise attacks. But the next spring, friendly Indians came to Plymouth. **Samoset** (SAM-oh-set) was the first Indian the Pilgrims met. He already spoke some English. His companion **Squanto** (SKWAN-toe) spoke English well.

The Indians taught the Pilgrims many things about life in the new land. They showed them how to plant corn, pumpkins, and squash. These were vegetables the settlers did not have in England. The Indians told the Pilgrims about the best places to hunt and fish.

13

In the fall of 1621, the Pilgrims had a good harvest. It looked like the next winter would be an easier one. The Pilgrims had built houses to protect them from the cold and wind. And they had enough food to last until spring. Everything was much better than it had been the winter before. The Pilgrims had great feelings of joy and thankfulness.

William Bradford, leader of the settlers, declared the first Thanksgiving Day in the fall of 1621. It was to be observed with prayer and a harvest feast.

The idea of a festival at harvest time is older than any holiday we celebrate, including Thanksgiving.

The Pilgrims also wanted to show their friendship for their Indian neighbors. And they were grateful to the Indians for all they had taught them. Because of this, the Pilgrims invited **Massasoit** (MASS-uh-soyt), chief of the **Wampanoag** (WOM-puh-nog) tribe to the feast.

Chief Massasoit came with ninety of his braves.
They brought five deer to the feast. The forests
around Plymouth were full of deer. Deer meat,
called **venison** (VEN-iss-un), was roasted over
the open fires. The men of Plymouth went out with
their guns and shot wild turkeys. At that time,
these American birds were plentiful. Now wild
turkeys are rare and are protected by law.

Oysters and clams were found at the seashore.
Pumpkins were cooked in pies and bread was
baked. Vegetables such as carrots, beans, corn,
and onions were served.

16

Because so many Pilgrims had died during the first winter, there were only five women to do all the cooking and baking for the first Thanksgiving. The cooking was done outdoors over open fires. And the meal was served outside at long, rough plank tables. There were so many people that some of the Pilgrims and their Indian guests had to sit on the ground.

To the Pilgrims the first Thanksgiving meal meant many things. The harvest was safely gathered and there was reason to rejoice. There would be more than enough food to last until spring. Then new crops could be planted.

The harvest feast was also the last big meal of the season. In the winter months food would not be plentiful. There would be no fresh vegetables. In those days food had to be eaten fresh or it had to be salted or dried to keep it from spoiling. Food could not be kept in refrigerators because there were none! Carrots, cabbages, and onions were kept in a storage place called a "cold cellar" or "root cellar." This was a little room where things might be kept cool and fresh longer.

We are used to a variety of foods all year long. But the earliest settlers did not even have apples, pears, or peaches. Nuts, berries, grapes, and plums were about the only fruits the Pilgrims had during their first years in the New World.

The Pilgrims had brought pigs and chickens with them on the *Mayflower*. But they did not have cows. Until cows were brought from England, the Pilgrims did not have beef, milk, or butter.

The first Thanksgiving feast lasted three days. This was a time of prayer, games, and songs. The Indians danced and wrestled. Captain Myles Standish, the military leader of the Pilgrims, drilled his soldiers.

The first Thanksgiving was a great success. But there was not a celebration every autumn. The year 1622 was a hard one. No feast was held, because there was little to celebrate. In 1623, the harvest was good again, so there was a celebration.

It is only from the year 1636 on that we have a complete record of a harvest festival and day of thanksgiving held each year.

By the late 1600s, November 25 had become the date for the yearly day of Thanksgiving in Massachusetts. Sometimes other places chose their own dates. But for more than two hundred years Thanksgiving was celebrated mainly in New England and in places where New Englanders had settled.

By about 1860, Thanksgiving was observed in all but two of the states. Each year the date was set by the governor of the state.

Mrs. Sara Josepha Hale wanted the entire country to celebrate Thanksgiving Day. She wrote letters to important people, and then she visited President Abraham Lincoln. Lincoln liked what Mrs. Hale wanted to do. In 1863, during the Civil War, he made Thanksgiving a national holiday. Lincoln hoped that the idea of Thanksgiving might help to unite the country.

Lincoln decided that Thanksgiving should be celebrated on the fourth Thursday of November. This was about the same time as the first Pilgrim Thanksgiving. In 1939, President Franklin D. Roosevelt changed the date for Thanksgiving to the next-to-last Thursday in November. For two years that was the date. But in 1941, Congress again made Thanksgiving the fourth Thursday in November, and it has stayed on this day.

For us, Thanksgiving Day is a happy time when we look forward to a delicious meal served in good company. From home to home the food may be different. But roast turkey, cranberry sauce, and pumpkin pie are almost always served, just as they were at the earliest Thanksgivings. The turkey may be stuffed with a dressing made from chestnuts, sausages, or oysters. Many southern cooks use cornbread stuffing.

Half the fun of Thanksgiving is waiting eagerly for the meal to be served. You can help by setting the table or making a centerpiece. A hollow pumpkin may be used instead of a bowl. You can fill it with colorful leaves or flowers like **chrysanthemums** (kris-AN-thuh-mumz).

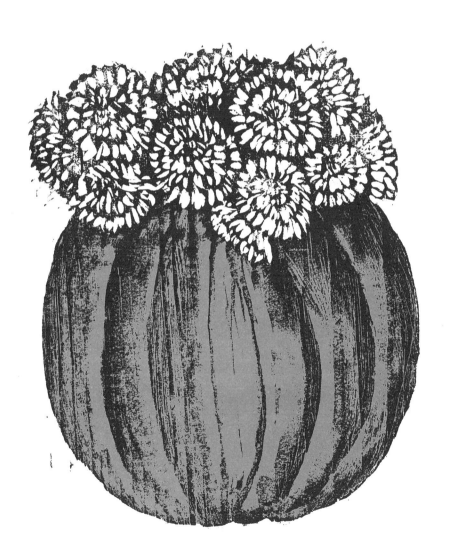

Pumpkins or wheat sheaves make good Thanksgiving decorations. Sometimes in churches and homes you will see a basket shaped like a cone lying on its side. This basket is called a **cornucopia** (kor-new-KO-pee-a). Often it is filled with grapes, nuts, and other fruits. The name comes from Latin and means "horn of plenty."

27

In many cities there are big Thanksgiving Day parades. Macy's Department Store has held its parade in New York City for over fifty years. Workers spend months making beautiful floats and huge balloons of cartoon characters. Perhaps you have watched the parade on television.

After Thanksgiving dinner is over, you can pitch in
to help clean up. In the afternoon, you can watch
football games or special holiday programs on
television. In the evening it is fun for grown-ups
and children to tell stories or to play games and
sing songs. "Over the River and Through the
Woods" is a favorite song that tells us about
Thanksgivings of olden times.

In many places, special religious services are held on Thanksgiving Day or on the night before. Sometimes at these services, people of many different faiths worship together. It is good to remember that we are all thankful for our many blessings.

INDEX

32